Contents

Preface

Antibiotics are probably the most important single discovery for medicine. Almost immediately after their clinical introduction the threat of mortality and morbidity caused by bacterial infection was considerably reduced. However, antibiotics are also among the most abused pharmaceuticals, with scant regard often being paid to the consequences of poor or inappropriate prescribing. Indeed there are increasing predictions that unless we moderate our use of these drugs bacterial resistance will eventually render them useless. As there are no serious contenders to take the place of antibiotics, it is essential for modern medicine that their efficacy is preserved.

This book is intended to allow the general prescriber to understand how antibiotics work, to demonstrate where they might be most appropriate and to make clear the threat of antibiotic resistance.

Antimicrobial Chemotherapy
Theory, Practice and Problems

Sebastian G B Amyes PhD DSc FRCPath
Christopher J Thomson PhD
Rex S Miles MB ChB FRCPath

*Scottish Antibiotic Reference Laboratory
Molecular Chemotherapy Unit
Department of Medical Microbiology
University of Edinburgh Medical School
Edinburgh, UK*

Glenn Tillotson MSc

*Scientific Affairs Department
Bayer Corporation
West Haven, Connecticut, USA*

Provided with an educational grant from

MARTIN DUNITZ

Although every effort has been made to ensure that the drug doses and other information are presented accurately in this publication, the ultimate responsibility rests with the prescribing physician. Neither the publishers nor the authors nor Bayer plc can be held responsible for errors or for any other consequences arising from the use of information contained herein.

The opinions expressed in this book are those of the authors and are not necessarily those of Bayer plc.

© Martin Dunitz Ltd 1996

First published in the United Kingdom
in 1996 by
Martin Dunitz Ltd
The Livery House
7– 9 Pratt Street
London NW1 0AE

A CIP record for this book is available from the British Library.

ISBN 1-85317-399-1

Printed and bound in Spain by Cayfosa

Selective toxicity

The essential property of an antimicrobial drug that equips it for systemic use in treating infection is selective toxicity. This means that the drug must inhibit the micro-organisms at lower concentrations than those that produce toxic effects in humans. Some antimicrobials can be given in very high doses without toxic effects (e.g. penicillins), but others may produce serious toxicity at levels that are not much above those required for treatment of infection; however, *no* antibiotic is completely safe.

Parenteral versus oral

Oral antibiotics have to be able to survive the acid conditions in the stomach. To achieve this, they may either be inherently resistant to destruction by acid or have functional groups added to form an ester, such as cefuroxime axetil. The ester is then cleaved, often by enzymes in the host, to release the pure antibiotic. The advantages of oral administration are its ease and its reduced cost. The disadvantage is that the drug has to undergo a circuitous route to reach the site of infection. Inevitably some antibiotic passes to the lower bowel, where some of the highest concentrations of bacteria in the body are found. This may cause destruction of the commensal faecal flora and lead to side-effects such as diarrhoea. It also provides a fertile breeding ground for resistance.

Short and long half-lives

The half-lives of early antibiotics were quite short, perhaps only one hour, so the antibiotics had to be administered many times per day. With oral versions, this causes problems with patient compliance, and with parenteral versions, it becomes expensive in resources. Increasingly, the newer antibiotics have much longer half-lives, some up to 33 hours. This means that the patient needs to be dosed just once a day in order to maintain sufficient drug concentrations.

Broad-spectrum and narrow-spectrum antimicrobial drugs

Antimicrobial drugs are often described as broad- or narrow-spectrum, according to the range of bacterial species that will be inhibited at standard therapeutic concentrations of the drug. However, no drug is specific for a particular pathogen and there will always be some effect on other bacteria. A narrow-spectrum antibiotic is usually preferable where the infecting species has been identified, but broad-spectrum cover may be desirable if the infecting organism has not yet been identified and therapy has to be started urgently.

Bactericidal and bacteriostatic antimicrobial action

Antimicrobial drugs may be bactericidal – they kill the bacteria – or predominantly bacteriostatic – they inhibit replication of the bacteria, which remain viable and may start to grow when the concentration of drug falls. Bactericidal drugs are usually preferable to bacteriostatic drugs, especially in immunosuppressed patients, but the decisive factor in evaluating an antimicrobial drug is experience of its efficacy in clinical practice. The most important factor in the cure of infection is the patient's own defence system; antibiotics cannot cure or prevent infection in the absence of adequate numbers of functional white cells in the blood. Bacteriostatic drugs may well be able to arrest the growth of the bacteria sufficiently for the patient's white cells to be able to eliminate the infection.

Combinations of antibiotics

Combinations of drugs may be used in order to prevent the emergence of drug-resistant strains, such as in the treatment of tuberculosis (see pages 32 and 47). This applies where there is an enclosed population of organisms and resistance is known to emerge during prolonged treatment of an individual patient. The same arguments do not apply where resistance arises in a population of organisms that are freely exchanged between different patients and healthy carriers.

There are many disadvantages in giving combinations of antimicrobial drugs when one drug would suffice. Some combinations of drugs can show antagonistic effects. In addition, fixed dosage ratios may apparently be convenient for administration, but do not permit the dosage of each drug to be adjusted independently. Although a broad spectrum of cover may be required initially, it is often possible to revert to a single narrow-spectrum agent once the nature of the infection has been ascertained.

Antimicrobial agents act in five ways:

- Inhibitors of cell wall synthesis
- Inhibitors of tetrahydrofolate synthesis
- Inhibitors of protein synthesis
- Inhibitors of DNA synthesis
- Inhibitors of RNA synthesis

Inhibitors of cell wall synthesis

The composition of the bacterial cell wall is unique in nature and agents which inhibit its production are therefore selective.

Vancomycin

Vancomycin is a glycopeptide antibiotic active against Gram-positive bacteria. It acts during the second stage of bacterial cell wall synthesis. By binding peptides containing D-alanyl-D-alanine, vancomycin prevents them interacting with the active site of the enzyme peptidoglycan synthetase, ultimately inhibiting the polymerization of UDP-N-acetyl-muramyl pentapeptide and N-acetylglucosamine into peptidoglycan.

Bacitracin

Bacitracin acts at stage two in cell wall synthesis by inhibiting conversion of phospholipid pyrophosphate to phospholipid, which is an essential reaction for the regeneration of the lipid carrier involved in cell wall synthesis.

β-lactams

The main examples are shown in Figure 1. All these antibiotics contain a β-lactam ring (shown by the arrow) and act in the final step of cell wall synthesis in which strands of peptidoglycan are cross-linked via peptide side chains. β-lactam antibiotics resemble the terminal D-alanyl-D-alanine of the pentapeptide and bind covalently to the active site of the transpeptidase enzyme, thereby inhibiting the transpeptidase step required for cross-linking the polysaccharide chains in cell wall peptidoglycan. β-lactams also interact with a number of other proteins at the cell membrane, called penicillin binding proteins (PBPs). The number and types of PBP in a cell varies among species. Some of the PBPs correspond to known enzymes involved in cell wall synthesis – others, however, have not been identified.

Penicillins
Natural penicillins (G and V) Penicillin G is the original penicillin. It is acid-labile and therefore must be administered by injection. It still remains the agent of choice in many cases for Gram-positive organisms. The drug has little activity against Gram-negative rods. Penicillin V – phenoxymethyl penicillin – is an acid-stable derivative of penicillin; it has much the same antibacterial spectrum as penicillin G but can be administered orally.

Penicillinase-resistant penicillins Methicillin is a semi-synthetic derivative of penicillin and was the first penicillin that was stable to staphylococcal β-lactamase. Methicillin is acid-labile so can only be administered by injection; flucloxacillin is similar to methicillin but is acid-stable and can be given orally.

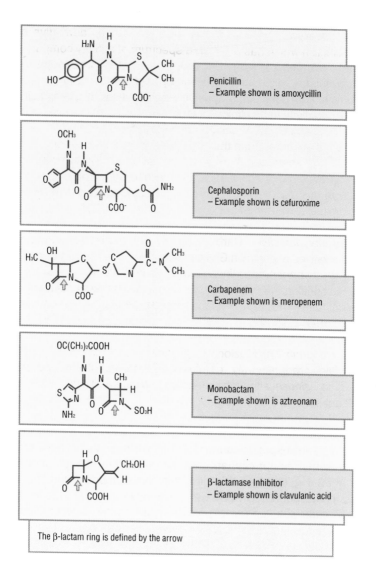

The β-lactam ring is defined by the arrow

Figure 1
Structures of the important β-lactam antibiotic groups.

Aminopenicillins Ampicillin is a semi-synthetic derivative of penicillin which has an altered spectrum of activity compared to penicillin. Ampicillin is active against many Gram-negative organisms which are unaffected by penicillin G. Although less active than penicillin G against Gram-positives, it retains sufficient activity to be clinically useful. Ampicillin is a broad-spectrum antibiotic which can be administered orally. However, it is poorly absorbed from the gut. Amoxycillin is a later derivative with the same spectrum of activity as ampicillin but with an improved pharmacokinetic profile, exhibiting better absorption from the gut which results in higher blood levels and lower residual levels in the gut.

Carboxypenicillins Carbenicillin and ticarcillin are carboxy derivatives of penicillin G. They show increased activity against *Pseudomonas aeruginosa*, which is intrinsically resistant to most β-lactam drugs, and activity against other ampicillin-resistant Gram-negative bacilli, such as *Proteus vulgaris* and *Enterobacter spp.*

Ureidopenicillins Mezlocillin, azlocillin and piperacillin are again predominantly employed for their activity against *P. aeruginosa*, although mezlocillin and piperacillin can used to treat serious Gram-negative infections in general.

Cephalosporins
The cephalosporins contain a β-lactam ring that is attached to a six-membered cephem nucleus rather than the five-membered ring found in penicillins. This permits modification of the cephalosporin nucleus in two positions (rather than one as is the case with penicillins), thereby significantly increasing the scope for semi-synthetic derivatives that can be modified to give altered properties. Cephalosporins are normally classified in generations – unfortunately there is no standardization in this and agents classified as one generation by some authors may be classed as a different generation by others. Some of these agents are parenteral drugs and others are oral.

Carbapenems

The nucleus of the carbapenems is similar to that of penicillins, with a five-membered side ring, but differs in the replacement of sulphur by carbon. Carbapenems have the broadest spectrum of activity of any of the β-lactam family and are active against both Gram-positive and Gram-negative bacteria, aerobes and anaerobes.

Monobactams

Aztreonam is the only monobactam currently available for clinical use. It is only active against Gram-negative species and shows no activity against Gram-positive bacteria.

β-lactamase inhibitors

Increasing resistance as a result of β-lactamase production (see page 39) has led to the development of β-lactamase inhibitors. These are compounds which when co-administered with the β-lactam prevent inactivation by β-lactamases. Three β-lactamase inhibitors are available for clinical use:

- Clavulanic acid combined with amoxycillin or ticarcillin
- Sulbactam combined with ampicillin or cefaperazone
- Tazobactam combined with piperacillin

All these inhibitors contain a β-lactam ring and function in the same way, acting as suicide inhibitors that bind to the active site of the β-lactamases.

Inhibitors of tetrahydrofolate synthesis

Two groups of antibiotics act in this area: the sulphonamides and trimethoprim. Both are competitive inhibitors of enzymes in the bacterial metabolic pathway, synthesizing tetrahydrofolate. Sulphonamides are structural analogues of para-amino benzoic acid and inhibit dihydropteroate synthetase; trimethoprim inhibits dihydrofolate reductase (Figure 2). The sulphonamides are selective in their action because the reaction catalysed by dihydropteroate synthetase does not occur in mammalian cells, which utilize preformed folates. The reduction of dihydrofolate to tetrahydrofolate does occur in mammalian cells; however, trimethoprim is a selective inhibitor of bacterial dihydrofolate reductase and inhibits the mammalian enzyme 100 000-fold less efficiently than the bacterial enzyme.

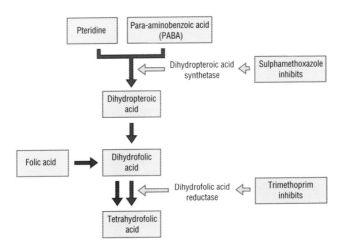

Figure 2
Action of co-trimoxazole. Metabolic pathway in bacteria is shown by red arrows and in man by blue arrows.

Because these two agents act on the same pathway, several claims have been made about the theoretical benefits of combining them. In particular, it was claimed that the two drugs acted together synergistically and that combined usage would delay the emergence of resistance. Thus when trimethoprim was first developed it was only available in combination with sulphamethoxazole (co-trimoxazole). However, trimethoprim alone is often as efficacious as this combination. The combination is recommended for some specific indications, such as *Pneumocystis carinii.*

Inhibitors of protein synthesis

There are a number of important groups of antibiotics that act on protein synthesis. The basis for selective activity in many but not all cases results from differences in structure between prokaryote and eukaryote ribosomes (Table 1).

Aminoglycosides

Aminoglycosides can be classified according to the structure of the aminocyclitol ring. There are three groups, typified by streptomycin, neomycin and kanamycin. Streptomycin interacts with the ribosomal 30S subunit. Neomycin and kanamycin also bind the 30S subunit but, in addition, appear to act elsewhere, including binding to the 50S ribosomal subunit. Interaction of aminoglycosides with bacterial ribosomes has a number of effects, including disruption of peptide chain formation and misreading of the genetic code. The resulting inadequate production of vital proteins has disruptive effects on many essential bacterial functions, leading to cell death. Streptomycin was the first of the aminoglycosides to be introduced into clinical use. Today the main four aminoglycosides are gentamicin, tobramycin, netilmicin and amikacin.

Macrolides

Erythromycin was the first of this group. It is a relatively narrow-spectrum drug with activity primarily against Gram-positive bacteria. Erythromycin is an inhibitor of protein synthesis, binding to a single site on the 50S ribosomal subunit. It is thought that this binding inhibits translocation by interfering with the association of peptidyl-tRNA after peptide bond formation. Erythromycin is primarily bacteriostatic in activity,

Antibiotic class	Representatives	Selective action	Metabolic effect
Aminoglycosides	Streptomycin Gentamicin Tobramycin Netilmicin Amikacin	Interaction with bacterial ribosomes but not mammalian ribosomes	Bactericidal
Macrolides and related compounds	Erythromycin Clarithromycin Azithromycin	Interaction with bacterial ribosomes but not mammalian ribosomes	Bacteriostatic
Tetracyclines	Tetracycline Oxytetracycline Doxycycline Minocycline	Inability of drug to be transported into mammalian cells	Bacteriostatic
Chloramphenicol	Chloramphenicol	Interaction with bacterial ribosomes but not mammalian ribosomes	Bacteriostatic
Lincomycins	Lincomycin Clindamycin	Interaction with bacterial ribosomes but not mammalian ribosomes	Bacteriostatic

Table 1
Inhibitors of protein synthesis.

although this is dose dependent and bactericidal activity can be observed at higher concentrations. Macrolides do not bind to mammalian ribosomes.

Tetracyclines

Tetracyclines inhibit protein synthesis as a result of binding to prokaryotic ribosomes. This interaction prevents the binding of amino-acyl-tRNA to the acceptor site on the mRNA ribosome, thus blocking the addition of new amino acids to the peptide chain. Tetracyclines also bind to mammalian ribosomes and the basis for their selective activity does not result from differential binding. The ability of tetracyclines to inhibit bacterial and not mammalian cells seems to result from an inability of the drug to enter mammalian cells. Tetracyclines exhibit a bacteriostatic effect on bacteria and have a broad spectrum of activity encompassing both Gram-negatives and Gram-positives, aerobes and anaerobes.

Lincomycins

Two lincomycin antibiotics are available, lincomycin and clindamycin. Clindamycin is a synthetic derivative of lincomycin which is more active and has improved absorption from the gut. The lincomycins bind to the bacterial 50S ribosome. They appear to bind at the same site as chloramphenicol and the macrolides but the effect of the lincomycins is to prevent initiation of peptide chain formation. They are predominantly bacteriostatic drugs, although under certain conditions they can be bactericidal. They are active primarily against Gram-positive bacteria and anaerobes.

Chloramphenicol

Chloramphenicol interacts with the bacterial 50S ribosomal subunit, preventing protein synthesis by inhibiting peptide bond formation. The interaction of chloramphenicol with the ribosome affects the attachment of aminoacyl-tRNA, preventing these compounds reacting with peptidyl transferase and stopping peptide bond formation. Chloramphenicol is a bacteriostatic agent and has a broad spectrum of activity.

Inhibitors of DNA synthesis

Quinolones

The original quinolone antibacterial, nalidixic acid, has been in widespread clinical use since 1962. However, it is only in recent years that the full potential of these agents has been realized. The development of modern quinolones stems from the discovery that insertion of a fluorine at the six position of the base nucleus broadened the spectrum and increased the activity of these compounds (Figure 3). This led to the development of the modern fluorinated 4-quinolones which have antibacterial activities 1000-fold greater than that of nalidixic acid; these new agents were introduced into clinical medicine in the 1980s.

The quinolone antibacterials are bactericidal agents that are thought to kill bacteria by a number of distinct mechanisms. While the molecular basis for this is only now becoming clear, it seems that central to their killing action is the interaction of the quinolone with bacterial DNA gyrase. DNA gyrase consists of two A and two B subunits and is the enzyme responsible for supercoiling strands of DNA into the bacterial cell. Nalidixic acid interacts with the A subunit, while the newer quinolones appear to interact with both the A and B subunits. This interaction with DNA gyrase is responsible for the lethal effects of

Figure 3
Chemical structure of ciprofloxacin.

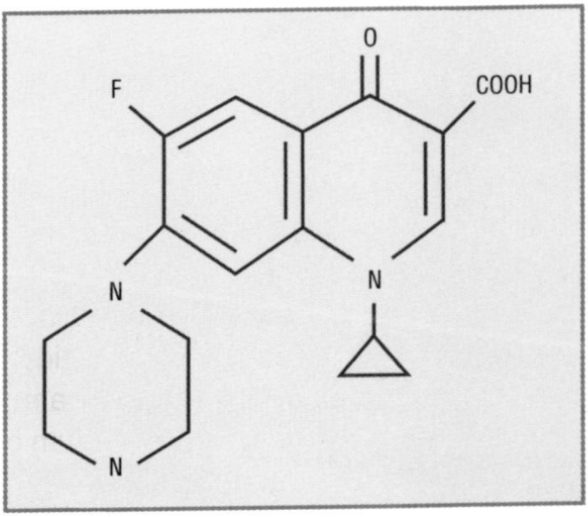

these drugs on bacteria. A variety of 4-quinolone drugs are available for clinical use; they all have a broad spectrum of activity although they are of limited value against some Gram-positive organisms.

Metronidazole

Originally metronidazole was solely an anti-fungal agent. Although not a classic inhibitor of DNA synthesis, it is included in this section as its bactericidal activity is mediated by its effects on DNA. Once metronidazole has entered the bacterial cell it undergoes reductive activation in which the nitro group of the drug is reduced by low redox potential electron transport proteins. The resulting active compounds damage the cell through interaction with DNA. The activity of metronidazole is restricted to anaerobic bacteria and it is the agent of choice for many anaerobic infections.

Inhibitors of RNA synthesis

Only one medically important antibiotic acts by directly inhibiting RNA synthesis. Rifampicin acts by inhibiting bacterial RNA polymerase. The importance of this antibiotic lies in the fact that it is one of the cornerstones in the treatment of tuberculosis (see page 49).

Summary of chemotherapeutic agents

(note — not all these agents are available in the United Kingdom)

Inhibitors of cell wall synthesis

β-lactams		
Benzylpenicillins	Penicillin G	
Phenoxypenicillins (oral penicillins)	Penicillin V	
Penicillinase-resistant penicillins (antistaphylococcal penicillins)	Oxacillin Cloxacillin Dicloxacillin	Methicillin Nafcillin
Aminopenicillins	Ampicillin	Amoxycillin
Carboxypenicillins	Carbenicillin	Ticarcillin
Ureidopenicillins (extended spectrum penicillins)	Azlocillin Mezlocillin	Piperacillin
Cephalosporins (1st generation)	Cephalothin Cefazolin Cephapirin Cephradine	Cephalexin Cephadroxil Cefaclor
(2nd generation)	Cephamandole Cefuroxime Cefonicid Ceforanide	Cefoxitin Cefmetazole Cefotetan Cefuroxime axetil
(3rd generation)	Cefotaxime Ceftriaxone Ceftizoxime Ceftazidime	Cefaperazone Moxalactam Cefixime
(4th generation)	Cefepime	Cefpirome
Monobactams	Aztreonam	

Cont'd.

| Carbapenems | Imipenem | Meropenem |
| β-lactamase inhibitors | Clavulanic acid
Sulbactam | Tazobactam |
| Other agents | Vancomycin | Bacitracin |

Inhibitors of protein synthesis

| Aminoglycosides | Streptomycin
Gentamicin
Tobramycin | Netilmicin
Amikacin |
| Macrolides | Erythromycin
Clarithromycin | Azithromycin |
| Tetracyclines | Tetracycline
Oxytetracycline | Doxycycline
Minocycline |
| Lincomycins | Clindamycin | Lincomycin |
| Other agents | Chloramphenicol | |

Inhibitors of tetrahydrofolate synthesis

| Sulphonamides | Sulphamethoxazole
Sulphadiazine | Sulphanilic acid |
| Diaminopyrimidines | Trimethoprim
Brodimoprim | Tetroxaprim |
| Combinations | Co-trimoxazole | |

Inhibitors of DNA synthesis

Quinolones	Nalidixic acid
Fluoroquinolones	Ciprofloxacin Enoxacin Norfloxacin Ofloxacin Sparfloxacin
Metronidazole	Metronidazole

Inhibitors of RNA synthesis

Rifampicin	Rifampicin

Pharmacokinetics applied to antimicrobials

The use and application of pharmacokinetic principles to antimicrobial agents is a rapidly growing science. The term pharmacokinetics is used to define the time course of drug absorption, distribution, metabolism and excretion. One of the main applications of clinical pharmacokinetics is to increase the effectiveness or to decrease the toxicity of a specific drug therapy. The term pharmacodynamics refers to the relationship between drug concentration at the site of action and phamacological response. However, when these principles are applied to antimicrobial therapy there are a number of factors which can alter the predicted outcome (Table 2).

The way in which the body copes with a drug is complex, involving several processes that work together to affect how much of a drug gets where in the body and at what concentrations. In order to understand these processes, a model of the body can be used. Such models are classified by the number of compartments needed to describe how a drug behaves in the body. There are one, two and multi-compartment models; these refer to groups of similar tissues or fluids. These models can be used to predict the time course of drug concentrations in the body. The highly perfused organs (e.g. heart, liver and kidneys) are considered to be one compartment (central) while fat, muscle, cerebrospinal fluid and so on are in the peripheral compartment.

Bacterial	Pharmacokinetics
Inhibitory activity Subinhibitory activity Concentration-dependent activity Time-dependent activity Bactericidal/bacteriostatic activity Post-antibiotic effect Resistance – phenotypic – transferability	Absorption Distribution Metabolism Excretion Protein-binding

Table 2
Factors which can influence therapeutic outcome.

There are several other key terms which are useful in understanding drug distribution. An important indicator of the extent of distribution is the volume of distribution (VoD). This relates the amount of drug in the body to the measured concentration in the plasma. A large volume of distribution indicates that the drug distributes extensively into body tissues and fluids. It does *not* specify which tissues or fluids.

$$\text{Volume of distribution} = \frac{\text{Amount of drug given (dose)}}{\text{Initial drug concentration}}$$

Other key aspects of drug handling include:

Clearance This is the removal of drug from plasma and relates the rate at which a drug is given and eliminated to the resultant plasma levels. It is expressed as volume/time.

C_{max} The maximum concentration reached at the site of infection, usually taken as the peak serum level.

t_{max} The time taken, after dosage, to reach the C_{max}.

Half-life (t½) The time taken for the concentration of the drug in the plasma to decrease by half. This is often used as an indicator as to how often the drug should be administered.

Area under the curve (AUC) The parameter which links clearance to dosing (Figure 4). It is easily calculated:

$$AUC = \frac{\text{Initial concentration}}{\text{Elimination rate constant}}$$

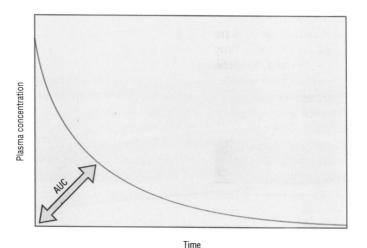

Time

Figure 4
Typical curve of antibiotic distribution.

Area under the inhibitory curve (AUIC) The extent of bacterial death with some antibiotics (e.g. 4-quinolones) is crucially dependent on the drug concentration. However, with other bacterial antibiotics (e.g. β-lactams) concentrations above four times the minimum inhibitory concentration (MIC) (see page 24) have no greater effect. With the latter group, the length of time that the drug concentration is above the MIC is usually the most important consideration. With the former group it is important to know the AUIC. This is an antimicrobial adaptation of AUC, and refers to the concentration of the drug which is able to exert antibacterial activity over a given organism for a specific time. The AUIC is the drug concentration divided by the minimium inhibitory concentration of a specific bacterial species. All AUIC values are reported for 24 hours of dosing. An AUIC of 125 is considered the lower limit of activity for a cure; the preferred value is ≥ 250.

Bearing these processes in mind, antimicrobials can be divided into those which have a high volume of distribution (e.g. quinolones) and those which need more regular dosing owing to short half-life (e.g. penicillins); by modifying the molecular structure of some drugs it has been possible to improve absorption and thus achieve better plasma concentrations (e.g. ampicillin to amoxycillin). Table 3 shows a selection of serum pharmacokinetics and other aspects of commonly used antimicrobials.

Antibiotic	Dose/route	Half-life	Protein-binding (%)	Bio-availability
Amoxicillin	0.5 g PO	0.8–2	20	80
Ampicillin	0.5 g PO 0.5 g IM	0.8–1.5	17–20	50
Penicillin	5 m Unit IV	0.5	40–60	20–30
Cefaclor	1 g PO	0.5–1.0	25	70
Cefixime	0.2 g PO	3–9	65	50
Ceftriaxone	1 g IM	8	83–95	–
Cefuroxime	1 g PO	1–2	33–50	36–50
Ciprofloxacin	0.5 g PO	3–6	40	60–80
Norfloxacin	0.4 g PO	2–4	10–15	30–40
Erythromycin	0.5 g PO	1.2–2.6	75–90	?
Metronidazole	0.5 g PO	6–12	<20	>80
Clindamycin	0.15 g PO	2–4	60–95	90

Table 3
Serum kinetics and other aspects of common antimicrobials.

The current drive with antimicrobial research is to develop agents which:

- Have a broad spectrum of antibacterial activity
- Are given once or twice a day (at the most)
- Have a large volume of distribution into specific tissues
- Are well tolerated

The principles of pharmacokinetics are being applied to achieve these aims.

Antimicrobials developed within the last ten years have shown some remarkable pharmacokinetic profiles. Agents belonging to the quinolone and macro/azalide classes have both high volumes of distribution and half-lives in excess of 5 hours (thus allowing once or twice-daily dosing). Among the cephalosporins, recent additions have included cefixime and ceftriaxone which have half-lives of 4 and 8 hours, respectively. A better understanding of aminoglycosides has allowed us to administer these drugs once a day as a bolus dose rather than three times daily as initially licensed. This shift has enabled these drugs to be used more safely without compromising their efficacy.

The concept of an agent continuing to exert its activity long after detectable concentrations have dispersed from the site of infection is known as post-antibiotic effect. It can be quantified by measuring the time that the recovering organism takes to multiply 10-fold. The longer this time, the greater the post-antibiotic effect. This varies between individual antimicrobials and different organisms. Nevertheless it is a useful indicator as to how long we can expect a drug to work beyond the actual dosing period.

In vitro tests are an invaluable guide in choosing therapy although they cannot always predict *in vivo* responses accurately; however, if an organism is found to be resistant to an antibiotic *in vitro* it is most unlikely that normal therapeutic doses of that antibiotic will be of value in eliminating the infection. There are essentially two methods of performing sensitivity tests in the laboratory – dilution tests and disk tests.

Dilution tests

Minimum inhibitory concentrations

These are performed with doubling dilutions of antibiotic solution in the bacterial culture medium. Tube dilution tests use a liquid culture medium; a known concentration of the drug is diluted in a series of doubling dilutions so that the range of concentrations of antibiotic obtained will cover the likely bactericidal and bacteriostatic levels of that antibiotic for the organism under test. Each tube is then seeded with a standard number of organisms and the tubes are incubated, usually overnight at 37°C. Control series of tubes should also be set up with standard organisms of known sensitivity as a check on the potency of the antibiotic preparation used and the accuracy of the dilution technique.

The **bacteriostatic** level of the antibiotic is read as the last tube showing no evident turbidity, i.e. the highest dilution (lowest concentration) of the drug that has inhibited growth of the organism. This bacteriostatic level indicates the minimal inhibitory concentration (MIC) of the antibiotic for that particular organism.

The **bactericidal** level is obtained by subculturing an inoculum from all tubes showing no turbid growth onto an agar medium, and this is incubated again. The last of the tubes yielding no growth on that agar indicates the minimum bactericidal concentration of the antibiotic (Figure 5).

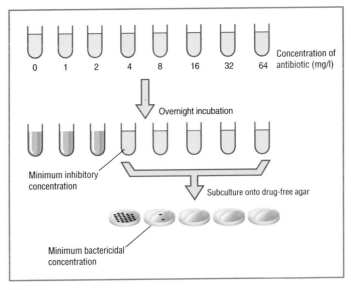

Figure 5
Tube dilution test for minimum inhibitory concentration (MIC) and minimum bactericidal concentration (MBC).

Sensitivity tests are usually set up with the antibiotic incorporated into solid media in agar plates. The test again aims to find the minimum concentration of antibiotic that inhibits visible growth. The advantage of using solid media is that many bacterial cultures can be tested on the same agar plate. Indeed, the plate may be read with a video camera and, with suitable software, the result can be incorporated straight into a database. There are also fewer problems with contamination (Figure 6).

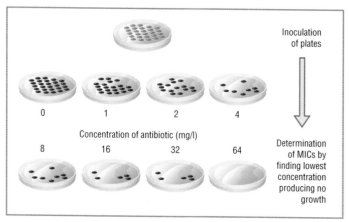

Figure 6
Agar dilution test for minimum inhibitory concentration (MIC).

Often it is important to know whether the whole bacterial population is sensitive or resistant. It is, therefore, convenient to describe a series of MIC results by the defined criteria of the range, the MIC_{50} and MIC_{90} values. These may be obtained by arranging the MIC results from the lowest to the highest. Some laboratories present their results as cumulative MICs, in which the MIC values tested are plotted against the percentage of bacteria inhibited by this concentration. However, the data are now usually entered into a database and this sorting can be conveniently performed by almost any database or spreadsheet computer programme.

Range

The range of MICs is simply the lowest and the highest MIC value in this series (Figure 7) and is often expressed as, for example, 1.0–512 mg/l. The range of MICs establishes the spread of the results and allows easy comparison of two populations. However, the range only shows the spread – it does not identify the distribution within that spread.

MIC$_{50}$

It is often convenient to know the median of the series (Figure 7), that is, the MIC value of the strain that appears halfway up the series. This MIC$_{50}$ figure will allow a broad comparison of the population with others. However, most MIC data are requested to establish whether resistance is a problem or is emerging, and the MIC$_{50}$ is too crude to establish this. When

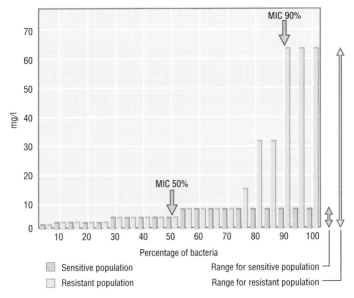

Figure 7
Cumulative MICs of a sensitive and resistant bacterial population, showing range, MIC$_{50}$ and MIC$_{90}$.

resistance emerges in a bacterial population it is often manifested by a few strains showing significant increases in MIC, whereas the rest of the population remains unaffected; here, a more significant measurement would be to determine the MIC_{90} value.

MIC_{90}

The MIC_{90} is the MIC value of the strain that appears 90% up the series (Figure 7). An antibiotic is likely to be considered successful if more than 90% of the population are inhibited by it, and the MIC_{90} value will show this readily. It will also show whether resistance is beginning to emerge in a population. Although emerging resistance will be reflected by an increase in the higher value of the range, the range will not show how many bacteria have decreased susceptibility. The MIC_{90} value will show when 10% are affected.

Breakpoints

Although the MIC determination may give the maximum information about bacterial sensitivity to antibiotics, for the routine laboratory it is both expensive and time-consuming. In order to be able to recommend the most suitable antibiotic, it is essential to know whether the causative organism is sensitive to the concentration of antibiotic at the site of infection. Thus a compromise version of the agar dilution MIC determination has been developed whereby the bacteria are tested against (usually) a single concentration of antibiotic. Sometimes, however, this may be extended and two distinct concentrations are used, a high value and a low value. The test is set up in exactly the same manner as the MIC determination, adhering to all the conditions about antibiotic concentrations, media, bacterial inocula, and so on (see above). The fixed concentrations of antibiotic may be provided by preparing suitable concentrations in the agar plate from stock solutions or, more usually, by placing an Adatab© in a fixed volume of media. The agar is inoculated as before by a multiple inoculator delivering 1–2 μl onto the surface of the agar plate. The plates are incubated and then examined. Essentially, the examination determines whether the bacterium has been inhibited, in which case is it is considered sensitive and suitable for treatment with this antibiotic, or whether the bacterium has grown, in which case it is considered resistant and unsuitable for treatment.

Choice of breakpoints

Recommendations for breakpoints are usually based on the C_{max} (the maximum concentration of antibiotic at the site of infection). This implies that breakpoints should be determined for every pathogen at every site of infection, but this is rarely the case. Sometimes two breakpoints are recommended, a low and a high. Usually a low breakpoint is one-quarter the C_{max} and the high breakpoint equals the C_{max}; this value is taken after the administration of a standard dose of antibiotic. The low breakpoint applies to normal doses for general infections and the high breakpoints apply to the designation 'intermediate sensitivity' (aminoglycosides, trimethoprim, quinolones), to increased dosage, or normal dosage when the antibiotic is concentrated locally (urinary tract).

The choice of breakpoints becomes particularly difficult when combinations of drugs are used. The use of breakpoints infers that the C_{max} and half-lives of the component parts of the drug combination will be very similar; however, in practice this is highly unlikely. The two drug combinations most often tested in the United Kingdom (but not the USA) are co-trimoxazole (trimethoprim and sulphamethoxazole) and co-amoxiclav (amoxycillin and clavulanic acid).

Disc sensitivity tests

Many diagnostic bacteriology laboratories use disc sensitivity tests; these give a rapid indication of the sensitivity or resistance of infecting organisms when the greater precision of tube dilution testing is not required.

This technique uses filter paper discs containing a known amount of antibiotic. The discs are usually coloured or printed with code letters to allow easy identification. The discs are placed carefully on a plate that has previously been seeded with the organism to be tested. After incubation overnight, the plate is examined for zones of inhibition of growth around the discs where the antibiotic has diffused into the medium.

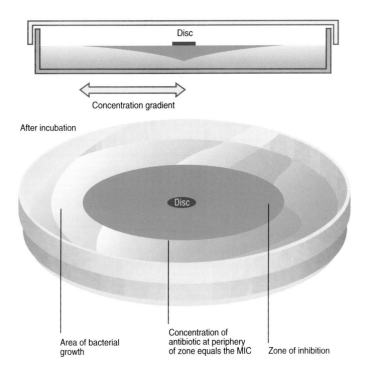

Figure 8
Diffusion of antibiotic from a paper disc.

The size of the zone of inhibition depends on the sensitivity of the organism and the rate of diffusion of antibiotic from the disc (Figure 8). The amount of a particular antibiotic put into a disc used for diagnostic bacteriology is such that a good zone of inhibition indicates a sensitive organism and no zone, or only a small zone, indicates a resistant organism. In other words, the disc test seeks to give a prediction of the likely response of the test organism to a particular antibiotic *in vivo*.

In diagnostic bacteriology it is important to be able to report to the clinician as rapidly as possible. It is usually possible to seed a plate with the infected sample (pus, urine, etc.), and add discs directly to it in order to have sensitivity test results available at the same time as the infecting organism is isolated. This procedure is inevitably less accurate than disc or tube tests using standard inocula of pure cultures, but if the results are interpreted with due caution they are of great value in giving early guidance to the clinician.

Genetics of antibiotic resistance

Bacteria may be naturally resistant to particular antibiotics – for example, the enterobacteria are not effectively inhibited by standard concentrations of benzylpenicillin. However, this inherent resistance has not traditionally been of great concern because the choice of antibiotic used takes it into account. Of more immediate importance clinically is the acquisition of resistance by sensitive pathogens. The mechanisms by which drug resistance may be acquired are:

- Chromosomal mutation and selection
- Transfer of plasmid-borne resistance (usually by conjugation)
- Transposition
- Integrons

Chromosomal mutation and selection

Drug resistance may arise within a culture or bacterial colony by the selection of spontaneously occurring mutants that are resistant to increased concentrations of a particular drug (Figure 9). This may occur in a single large step, with the cell acquiring resistance to high levels of the drug in a single mutation (e.g. streptomycin or erythromycin), or it may require multiple small steps with sequential selection, gradually building up the level of resistance until it becomes high enough to be of clinical significance (e.g. tetracycline).

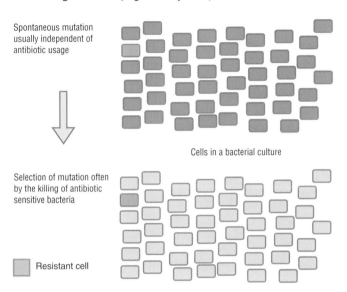

Spontaneous mutation usually independent of antibiotic usage

Cells in a bacterial culture

Selection of mutation often by the killing of antibiotic sensitive bacteria

Resistant cell

Figure 9
Chromosome mutation – selection of a resistant variant.

Transfer of plasmid-borne resistance

Plasmid-mediated resistance generally causes much greater concern. In the Gram-negative rods, conjugation allows spread of R plasmids (plasmids bearing drug-resistance genes) between cells of a wide range of different strains and species of Gram-negative bacilli. Transfer occurs fairly readily among the enterobacteria – *Escherichia coli*, *Klebsiella* spp, *Proteus* spp, *Salmonella* spp and *Shigella* spp. These coliform plasmids may also be transferred to less closely related genera *in vitro*, e.g. *Pseudomonas* spp, *Vibrio* spp or *Yersinia* spp. R plasmid resistance is common in *Pseudomonas aeruginosa* and there is some exchange of R plasmids between *Pseudomonas* spp and the enterobacteria. Most clinically important drug resistance in these bacteria is found to be plasmid borne and transferred by conjugation (Figure 10).

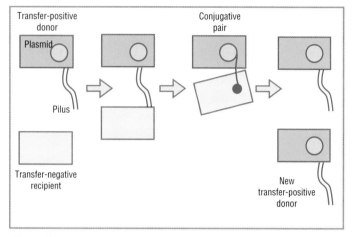

Figure 10
Stages of conjugation in Gram-negative bacteria.

Detection of plasmid transfer

Plasmid transfer is usually an infrequent event and thus detection of the transconjugant requires positive selection. This is often achieved by the use of recipient bacteria that are resistant to antibiotics for which plasmid transfer has never been detected (rifampicin, nalidixic acid). The donor and the recipient bacteria are mixed together for a fixed time period, often 1 hour. At the end of the conjugation, the mixture is placed onto selective agar plates containing two antibiotics; the first is the antibiotic for the transferable resistance gene and the second is the antibiotic to which the recipient is resistant. Controls are set up with the donor and recipient on the same selective media. The selective plates are incubated and transconjugants identified by growth on the selective plates inoculated with the conjugation mixtures, provided that there is no growth on the control plates.

Transposition

The obvious chromosomal origin of several plasmid-mediated resistance genes, and the widespread occurrence of many different resistance genes within a variety of bacterial genera, suggest that mechanisms must exist which enable the mobilization of resistance genes from their original location to new genetic locations within clinical bacteria. The discovery of insertion sequences (IS), and subsequently of transposons, provides one explanation whereby genes can be 'picked up' and moved independently to new sites. These new sites can be within the same or an alternative replicon in the original cell (Figure 11).

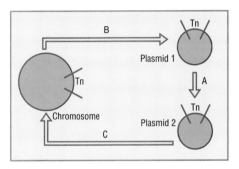

A: Plasmid to plasmid
B: Chromosome to plasmid
C: Plasmid to chromosome

Figure 11
Transposition (Tn) resistance — migration of a cluster of resistance genes.

Transposons, like the smaller IS elements from which they derive, possess the ability to transpose from one DNA molecule (the donor) to another (the recipient) but are themselves unable to replicate independently. A large number of transposons and IS elements have been described in both Gram-negative and Gram-positive bacteria and the genetic basis of transposition has been elucidated for several of these. All transposons, with only one or two exceptions, are characterized by the presence of transposase genes whose products act on inverted repeat sequences found at the ends of the transposable element. Thus the features essential for transposition are: inverted repeat sequences at the left and right ends of the transposon which function in *cis* (on the same section of DNA), and at least one transposase enzyme which may function in *trans* (in unrelated DNA molecules) for some transposons.

Integrons

A new type of genetic element has been described recently in the plasmids and transposons of Gram-negative bacteria. This element, called an integron, is characterized by conserved 5′ and 3′ ends which flank a variable central DNA segment. The 5′ conserved end contains a functional gene coding an enzyme, integrase, which mediates site-specific integration of external DNA, often containing a resistance gene, into the integron. The integron usually resides within a transposon (Figure 12). Essentially, the integron extracts segments of DNA from other replicons – therefore, the antibiotic resistance genes carried by a transposon that possesses an integron vary depending on which resistance genes it has poached from other replicons. In Figure 12, the transposon on plasmid 2 pos-

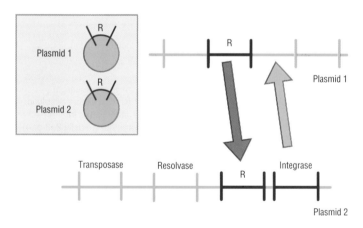

Figure 12
Integron resistance — poaching of resistance genes. The integrase gene of plasmid 2 excises the resistance gene (R) of plasmid 1 and inserts it next to the integrase gene. Therefore both plasmids now have copies of the gene.

sesses an integron. This integron produces an enzyme (integrase) which interacts with plasmid 1 and randomly extracts DNA from it. If it extracts a complete resistance gene, the transposon will now confer resistance to that antibiotic. If the host bacterium is challenged with that antibiotic, then the integron will provide a selective advantage on the cell.

Mechanisms of antibiotic resistance

The main mechanisms of resistance are:

1. Impermeability	The antibiotic fails to get into the bacterial cell or is removed from the bacterial cell faster than it can enter
2. Destruction	The antibiotic is destroyed so that the active drug is no longer intact and thus cannot attack its normal target
3. Modification	The antibiotic is modified so that the active drug is no longer intact and thus cannot attack its normal target
4. Alteration of target	The target of the antibiotic is modified so that the drug can no longer bind to it
5. Additional target	A second target is produced which is usually less sensitive to binding by the antibiotic and thus provides a by-pass to the original inhibition
6. Hyperproduction of target	The target is produced in larger quantities than normal, thus the excess target molecules mop-up the available antibiotic. This mechanism often occurs in conjunction with another (usually 2, 3 or 4)

If the resistance has arisen from chromosomal mutation, then all of the resistance mechanisms could, in theory, be employed. If, on the other hand, the resistance is determined by plasmid, transposon or integron genes, the options are more limited because the resistance mechanism usually has to be a single gene product and it has to be dominant within the cell. Examples are shown in Table 4.

Resistance mechanism	Chromosome	Plasmids, transposons and integrons
Impermeability	Most antibiotics	Tetracycline Chloramphenicol
Destruction	β-lactams	β-lactams
Modification	Aminoglycosides	Aminoglycosides Chloramphenicol
Alteration of target	Aminoglycosides Trimethoprim	Macrolides
Additional target	Trimethoprim Sulphonamides	Trimethoprim Sulphonamides
Hyperproduction of target	Trimethoprim	Trimethoprim (coupled with additional target)

Table 4
Mechanisms of antibiotic resistance.

Impermeability

This is a relatively common mechanism of inherent resistance. The antibiotic just cannot penetrate the cell sufficiently to attack the target. *Pseudomonas aeruginosa* has very few porins on its outer membrane and thus antibiotics generally have difficulty in penetrating the cell.

On the other hand, impermeability is quite a rare mechanism of chromosomal mutational resistance because the changes required to provide impermeability are often very energy-dependent, which puts the cell at a significant disadvantage. However, chromosomal mutational resistance to tetracycline is provided by impermeability. This large antibiotic has to be actively transported into the bacterial cell. The mutation is simply an inactivation of the transport mechanism.

Plasmid-mediated resistance to tetracycline is also mediated by an impermeability-like mechanism. However, the plasmid does not interfere with the active transport of the antibiotic into the cell. Instead, it encodes a protein that expels the antibiotic out of the cell faster than it can get in. The dynamic equilibrium that this sets up ensures that there is insufficient tetracycline within the cell to interfere with bacterial protein synthesis. Like the mutational chromosomal mechanism, the plasmid impermeability-like mechanism only increases the resistance of the cell by between 10- and 100-fold and is often not efficient.

Destruction

The only example of this mechanism is that to β-lactam drugs (penicillins, cephalosporins and carbapenems); however, it is the most successful of the resistance mechanisms. It is manifested by the production of β-lactamases that can hydrolyse and inactivate various members of this family of antibiotics. The bond that all β-lactamases hydrolyse is shown by the arrows in Figure 1 (page 6).

The β-lactamase hydrolyses the carbon-nitrogen bond of the β-lactam ring. The integrity of this ring is crucial to the activity of the antibiotic. In Gram-positive bacteria, the β-lactamase is produced within the cytoplasm of the cell and is exported through the cell membrane into the surrounding medium, thus providing a drug-free blanket around the cell. It also provides protection for other micro-organisms in close proximity. In Gram-negative bacteria, the β-lactamase is again produced in the cytoplasm; however, most of it is exported only as far as the periplasmic space, between the two membranes. It is here that the β-lactamase intercepts and destroys the incoming β-lactam drug (Figure 13). This is a more directed and more efficient mechanism of destruction than that found in Gram-positive bacteria.

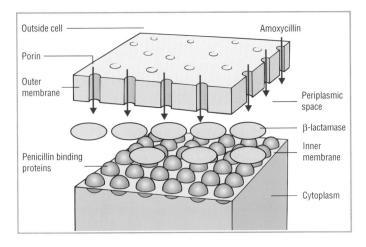

Figure 13
Interaction of amoxycillin with a β-lactamase in Gram-negative bacteria.

It has recently been reported that more than 200 β-lactamases have been found in clinical bacteria. They have conveniently been classified by their molecular structure into five groups (A – E). There is no homology between each group but significant homology exists within a group. In all β-lactamases, there is one main active site component; this can either be a serine molecule that provides the catalytic basis for the hydrolysis of penicillins and cephalosporins (classes A, C and D), or a metal ion that provides the catalytic basis for carbapenem hydrolysis (classes B and E).

Class A

The class A enzymes have been studied in most detail. They comprise the chromosomal β-lactamases of Gram-positive bacteria and the most common plasmid-encoded β-lacta-mases. In any study of plasmid-encoded, β-lactamase-conferred resistance performed anywhere in the world, at least 75% of all the enzymes will be the class A β-lactamase TEM-1. This enzyme is highly efficient at binding and hydrolysing amoxycillin, conferring high levels of resistance (MIC >1000 mg/l). β-lactamase inhibitors were developed specifically to overcome the effects of this enzyme. However, the β-lactamase has been able to mutate to prevent binding of the inhibitor. The cephalosporins have also been used to overcome the effect of the TEM-1 β-lactamase. Unfortunately, the TEM molecule has been able to mutate so that it can bind and hydrolyse the most sophisticated cephalosporins.

Classes B and E

The class B and E enzymes are metallo-β-lactamases, most notably active against the carbapenems, such as imipenem and meropenem. They are usually encoded by the bacterial chromosome and have to be induced in order to produce sufficient enzyme to confer resistance. Even elevated levels may be insufficient to confer resistance and this type of β-lactamase has to operate alongside another resistance mechanism, such as reduced permeability. A very limited number of class B β-lactamases have been found to be plasmid-mediated and these are not inducible but are constitutively produced.

Class C

The class C β-lactamases are predominantly the chromosomally-encoded β-lactamases of Gram-negative rods. The production of these β-lactamases also has to be induced to produce sufficient enzyme (Figure 14). Induction is not a very efficient long-term mechanism and the host bacteria are more successful if the repression system is completely disabled. Thus de-repression occurs with a mutation in the repressor gene so that no repressor protein is produced. This is a stable change and can only be reversed with a back mutation.

A very small number of class C β-lactamase genes have been found on plasmids (e.g. BIL-1 and MIR-1). When this occurs, only the β-lactamase gene is present; there is no repression system so the gene is expressed constitutively.

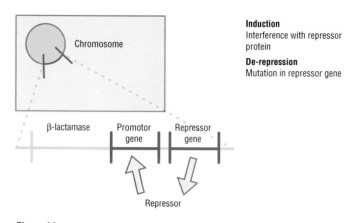

Induction
Interference with repressor protein

De-repression
Mutation in repressor gene

Figure 14
Chromosomal class C β-lactamase production in Gram-negative bacteria showing the role of a cytoplasmic repressor.

Class D

The class D β-lactamases are mainly plasmid-encoded and predominantly act against penicillins. Their origin remains unknown but they are found in a diversity of bacterial species.

Modification

Modification of an antibiotic has the same effect as destruction in that an inactive drug is created which can no longer inhibit its target. Essentially the plasmids encode a gene that adds a functional group to the antibiotic. The enzyme can have one of three actions:

Acetyl-transferase	The enzyme adds an acetyl group
Adenyl-tranferase	The enzyme adds an adenyl group
Phospho-transferase	The enzyme adds an phosphate group

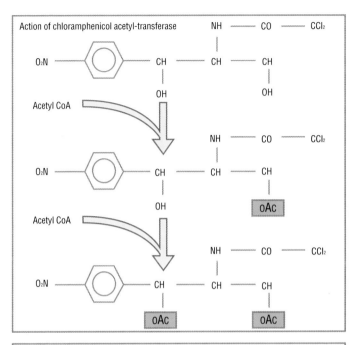

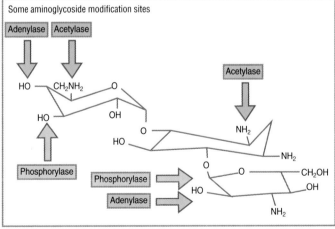

Figure 15
Sites of modification by adenyl-, acetyl-, and phospho-transferases to render aminoglycosides inactive and confer resistance to the host bacterium.

The main antibiotics that are modified in this manner are chloramphenicol and the aminoglycosides. Chloramphenicol can only have acetyl groups added and this is obtained from acetyl-CoA (Figure 15). Clinical bacteria can use all three actions against the aminoglycosides. Modifying enzymes are produced in the cytoplasm but often act at the point where the antibiotic enters the cell. In the case of the aminoglycosides, the antibiotics are actively transported into the cell and modified at their point of entry. Only a small proportion of the incoming antibiotic is modified (often around 1%), which suggests that the mechanism of resistance is manifested by the modified antibiotic blocking the transport system into the cell, rather than its inability to bind to the 30S ribosomal subunit. Modification produces moderately high levels of resistance on their host bacterium (MIC 100–500 mg/l).

Alteration of target

Alteration of target is the most common mechanism of chromosomal mutation of antibiotics such as the aminoglycosides. The target protein on the 30S ribosomal subunit alters so that it cannot bind the aminoglycoside. This produces very high levels of resistance (MIC >2000 mg/l).

The most studied examples of target alteration are the 4-quinolone resistant mutants. The target of the 4-quinolones, DNA gyrase, is composed of two pairs of subunits, A and B. Changes in the A subunit can be particularly effective in preventing 4-quinolones binding, thus conferring relatively high levels of resistance on the host bacterium (MIC >64 mg/l).

Alteration of target is the mechanism used for the plasmid-encoded resistance to the macrolides, such as erythromycin.

Additional target

This is usually a plasmid-mediated mechanism of resistance. The antibiotic binds to its normal target but the plasmid produces an additional target, which is less susceptible to the antibiotic. This mechanism of resistance can only work if the quantity required of the product of the inhibited step is low. This is the case for the co-factor tetrahydrofolate. Trimethoprim selectively inhibits bacterial dihydrofolate reductase (Figure 16) and the plasmid produces an additional dihydrofolate reductase that cannot readily bind the drug but can still reduce dihydrofolate to tetrahydrofolate. Often the plasmid-encoded enzyme binds the drug around 10 000-fold less effectively than the chromosomal enzyme and there is a corresponding increase in resistance on the host bacterium (MIC >1000 mg/l).

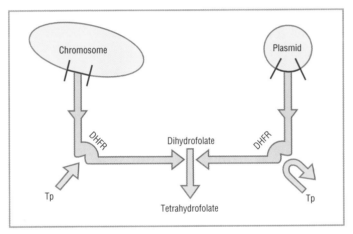

Figure 16
By-pass mechanism of plasmid-encoded trimethoprim resistance — production of an additional dihydrofolate reductase (DHFR).

Hyperproduction of target

Chromosomal dihydrofolate reductase can be hyperproduced by 100-fold so that it is able to bind many trimethoprim molecules. Even if 99% of the produced dihydrofolate reductase molecules are inhibited by trimethoprim, there are enough enzyme molecules to reduce dihydrofolate to provide sufficient tetrahydrofolate for the cell's needs. It is a highly expensive mechanism of resistance in terms of energy and the host cell has a selective disadvantage once the antibiotic has been removed.

Antimycobacterium therapy

The genus *Mycobacterium* contains over 40 species. Few, however, cause disease in humans. The most prevalent is *M. tuberculosis*, which is estimated to infect over 1.7 billion people – about a third of the world's population. Of these, around 8 million develop clinical disease each year. The so-called 'atypical' species that cause human disease include *M. kansasii, M. marinum, M. avium-intracellulare, M. fortuitum* and several others.

Tuberculosis has been a recognized clinical entity since ancient Greek times, killing young and old, the famous and not so famous. It is just over 100 years since Robert Koch published his treatise which linked the tubercule bacillus to the devastating disease. Within the last 40 years, considerable progress has been made in our knowledge of the pathogenesis, epidemiology, prevention and treatment of tuberculosis.

Anti-tubercle therapy has improved markedly since 1944, when it was discovered that streptomycin was effective in the treatment of human disease. Some five years later the combination of para-aminosalicylic acid (PAS) and streptomycin was demonstrated to be effective against streptomycin-resistant strains of *M. tuberculosis*, and this combination therapy approach became the mainstay of tuberculosis treatment programmes.

In the early 1950s isoniazid was shown to be active against *M. tuberculosis* and replaced PAS/streptomycin as the mainstay of treatment; its main benefit has been to shorten the course of therapy, which had been 12 months or longer in some patients.

In the 1960s new anti-tuberculosis agents were introduced; these included pyrazinamide, ethambutol and rifampicin. These drugs allowed shorter regimens and intermittent therapy. The latter approach has proven to be of particular value in developing nations, where supervised daily drug administration is not the norm.

Antimycobacterial agents

Streptomycin

Streptomycin is an aminoglycoside which can only be given parenterally. It acts on the protein synthetic pathway, in the growing phase of the bacterial lifecycle. Although it penetrates into the appropriate tissues, its toxic side-effects, particularly vestibular damage, mean that it is now used as a last-resort agent.

Para-aminosalicylic acid (PAS)

PAS is a foul-tasting drug with marked gastrointestinal side-effects, and is not in regular use today.

Isoniazid

Unusually, this drug is active only against tubercle bacilli. It is highly potent and bactericidal, and has become the mainstay of therapy due to its activity within the macrophage. It is well tolerated, penetrates well into tissues and is inexpensive. Isoniazid is given orally in a single dose and can achieve high peak concentrations. Adverse reactions are uncommon but include disturbances in liver enzymes, blurred vision, slurred speech and occasionally hepatitis (0.1%). Resistance is unusual but can develop if used as a single agent.

Pyrazinamide

This agent has a remarkable sterilizing effect on tubercle bacilli contained within the macrophage. It can be given orally, yielding high serum and CSF levels. Due to these factors it has found a place in short course regimens. Adverse reactions are unusual but include hepatic problems; dermal hypersensitivity and photosensitivity may also occur.

Ethambutol

Ethambutol has effectively replaced PAS as a combination agent for the treatment of both tubercle and other mycobacteria. It is a bacteriostatic agent which acts on growing organisms. After oral administration it achieves high serum and tissue levels. The major side-effect of ethambutol therapy is that of optic damage by a neuritis which affects visual acuity and colour vision. These changes are dose-dependent and normally reversible.

Rifampicin

This is a broad-spectrum antibacterial with potent activity against many Gram-positive species, such as staphylococci, as well as against mycobacteria. It has been shown to be of great value in primary therapy as well as relapse treatment. Side-effects associated with rifampicin include elevated liver enzymes, central nervous system disturbances, allergic reactions and – worrying to the patient but not clinically significant – orange colouration of saliva, sweat, tears, urine and stool. To date primary resistance is rare in the UK (<1%); however, care must be employed in its use as single step mutation can lead rapidly to development of resistance.

Other drugs

Other agents which may be used when primary or first-line therapy fails include ethionamide, prothionamide, cycloserine, kanamycin, capreomycin and thiacetazone. Each have significant disadvantages. New agents presently being investigated include ciprofloxacin, oxazolidinones and gangamicin as well as other, as yet unnamed, chemicals.

Treatment regimens

The standard treatment regimen for tuberculosis as recommended by the British Thoracic Society is shown in Table 5. Intermittent therapy is currently being evaluated – the idea behind this is that it leads to fewer adverse effects, leading in turn to better compliance with medication and an improved clinical and bacteriological result.

Drug	Initial phase (2 months)	Continuation phase (4 months)	Adverse reactions
Rifampicin	10 mg/kg/d	450–600 mg/d	Hepatitis, gastrointestinal upsets
Isoniazid	5 mg/kg/d	200–300 mg/d	Peripheral neuropathy, hepatitis
Pyrazinamide	30 mg/kg/d	1.5 –2 g/d	Gastrointestinal upsets
Ethambutol	15–25 mg/kg/d	–	Neuritis

Table 5
Standard treatment regimen for tuberculosis.

These therapeutic agents must *only* be instituted by an appropriately qualified physician following full clinical investigations to confirm the presence of acid-alcohol fast bacilli. The ability of mycobacteria to develop single or multiple resistance mechanisms is now the cause of major epidemics of multi-drug resistant tuberculosis (MDRTB) in the USA and South-East Asia. These outbreaks create huge infection control problems as presently there is no known effective treatment regimen – even cocktails of six or seven drugs are proving ineffective.

For the treatment of 'atypical' mycobacteria it is preferable to tailor the regimen to match the sensitivity pattern of the isolated strain. However, the atypical species frequently infect immuno-compromised patients, such as those with AIDS, and in these cases the instituted therapy may be in vain. For the immuno-competent patient, infections such as those caused by *M. marinum* ('fish-tank disease') are fairly easily, but lengthily, treated with conventional agents.

In the United Kingdom anti-tuberculosis therapy is still effective against the vast majority of the 6000 or so cases seen annually; however, with the threat of HIV and AIDS and the importation of multi-resistant strains from abroad, vigilance must be maintained.

Clinical use of antibiotics

The suggestions in the following lists are for initial treatment only. It is essential to seek specialist/microbiologist advice. Prescribers should attempt to tailor therapy to the needs of the individual patient. There is a complex interaction between patient, organism and antibiotic. The following points may be helpful:

1. Conform, as far as possible, with local prescribing policies and protocols
2. Be aware of local antibiotic sensitivity patterns
3. Advice regarding antibiotic prescribing is available from microbiologists, infectious disease specialists and clinical pharmacologists and pharmacists
4. Take microbiological specimens before starting treatment. When submitting specimens to laboratories, it is valuable to specify recent exposure to antibiotics and the empirical treatment which is to be given
5. Empirical therapy should be chosen with regard to likely pathogen, 'best guess' antibiotic (see 2), pharmacology of the agent and the possibility of drug toxicity or interaction (see 3)
6. Intravenous dosing is recommended for severely unwell patients. Whichever route is chosen, ensure that the dose and dose interval are appropriate and that the antibiotic is given at the correct intervals
7. Doses have not been included in these tables. Refer to the British National Formulary section 5 (antibiotics) and the various appendices for information on drug interactions, use in pregnancy and so on

8. Try not to use systemic antibiotics for topical treatment
9. Drainage of a collection of pus is usually more effective than antibiotic therapy

Urinary tract

Acute cystitis	Cephalexin **or** Trimethoprim **or** Amoxycillin **or** Co-amoxiclav **or** Ciprofloxacin or norfloxacin *Note* Approximately 40% of coliforms are resistant to amoxycillin and 20% to trimethoprim. Avoid use in complicated and recurrent urinary tract infection (UTI)
UTI with significant systemic upset	Ceftriaxone or cefotaxime **or** Co-amoxiclav **or** Gentamicin **or** Ciprofloxacin
Asymptomatic bacteriuria	Do not treat unless the patient is pregnant, diabetic, or has outflow obstruction, renal scarring or a previous history of pyelonephritis
Complicated and chronic infections (including catheterized patients)	Seek specialist advice. Treat infection in catheterized patients only if symptomatic

Ear, nose and throat infections

Acute otitis media	Co-amoxiclav **or** Cephalexin **or** Azithromycin
Acute mastoiditis	Co-amoxiclav **or** Ceftriaxone **or** Cefotaxime
Chronic otitis media/mastoiditis	Consult ENT surgeon Take bacteriological specimens
Dental and oral infection	Amoxycillin +/- metronidazole **or** Azithromycin +/- metronidazole **or** Co-amoxiclav
Nasal carriage of methicillin-resistant *Staphylococcus aureus*	Mupirocin 2% nasal ointment applied 3 times per day for no more than 5 days *Note* Consult Infection Control Team
Otitis externa	Local cleansing *Note* Consult ENT surgeon if the problem is not resolving. Topical aminoglycosides may cause drug-induced deafness
Sinusitis	Co-amoxiclav **or** Azithromycin **or** Ciprofloxacin
Sore throat (streptococcal)	Penicillin **or** Azithromycin

Respiratory system

Acute exacerbation of chronic bronchitis	Amoxycillin **or** Azithromycin **or** Co-amoxiclav **or** Ciprofloxacin

Aspiration pneumonia	Piperacillin/tazobactam **plus** gentamicin **or** Ciprofloxacin **plus** co-amoxiclav **or** Meropenem **plus** gentamicin
Bronchiectasis	Seek specialist advice
Cystic fibrosis	Seek specialist advice
Legionella pneumonia	Clarithromycin **plus** rifampicin
Pneumocystis	Seek specialist advice
Pneumonia	Co-amoxiclav **plus** clarithromycin
Severe pneumonia	Ceftriaxone or cefotaxime **plus** clarithromycin *or, if hospital acquired* Gentamicin **plus** clarithromycin **plus either** ciprofloxacin or ceftazadime or piperacillin/tazobactam
Staphylococcal pneumonia	Flucloxacillin **plus either** fusidic acid by mouth or gentamicin
Tuberculosis	Seek specialist advice

Conjunctival infections

Microbiological material should be taken for examination before antimicrobials are prescribed. Most episodes are self-limiting and require no treatment

Acute conjunctivitis	Gentamicin 0.3% drops **or** Chloramphenicol 0.5% drops *Note* 1. In severe infections consult ophthalmic surgeon 2. Patients with keratitis or endophthalmitis require urgent referral to an ophthalmic surgeon

Cont'd.

3. Treat chlamydial conjunctivitis with local tetracycline plus oral clarithromycin. Chloramphenicol drops may mask a chlamydial infection
4. Treat gonococcal infections with local lavage using saline, plus ceftriaxone as a single dose. In ophthalmia neonatorum prescribe ceftriaxone in a single dose (for premature infants or in those with elevated bilirubin levels use cefotaxime)

Skin and soft tissue infections

Animal bites	Benzylpenicillin **or** *for out-patients* Co-amoxiclav by mouth *Note* Consult microbiologist if patient hypersensitive to penicillins
Cellulitis	Benzylpenicillin **plus** flucloxacillin
Diabetic foot ulcers and other chronic superficial lesions	Treat on the results of bacteriological examination of **good** specimens
Erysipelas	Benzylpenicillin *Note* Consult microbiologist if patient hypersensitive to penicillins
Furuncles and carbuncles	Flucloxacillin **or** Clindamycin *Note* Consult Infection Control Team for patients with recurrent infections

Gas gangrene and clostridial cellulitis	Surgical and bacteriological opinion Benzylpenicillin **plus either** metronidazole or clindamycin
Human bites	Co-amoxiclav **or** Erythromycin **plus** metronidazole
Impetigo	Amoxycillin **plus** local antiseptics (e.g. povidone iodine) may be useful
Myositis	Surgical intervention Bacteriological opinion Antibiotic therapy on the basis of bacteriological findings but will usually include flucloxacillin +/- benzylpenicillin
Necrotising cellulitis and fasciitis (Streptococcal gangrene)	Surgical intervention Bacteriological opinion Benzylpenicillin **plus** clindamycin **plus** gentamicin
Progressive bacterial synergistic gangrene (Meleney's gangrene)	Surgical intervention Benzylpenicillin **plus** other antibiotics on the basis of bacteriological findings
Staphylococcal scalded skin syndrome (rare in adults)	Flucloxacillin Topical saline compresses
Toxic shock syndrome	Fluid replacement Removal of tampon if present Bacteriological opinion Flucloxacillin
Wound infections	Treat on the basis of bacteriological opinion/findings *Note* In many skin and soft tissue infections, surgical intervention, local toilet and tetanus prophylaxis may be of crucial importance

Gastrointestinal tract

Antibiotic-associated colitis/diarrhoea (*Clostridium difficile*)	Metronidazole **or** Vancomycin *for severely ill patients*
CAPD associated peritonitis	Seek specialist advice
Enteric fever and invasive salmonellosis	Consult infectious diseases specialist or microbiologist Ciprofloxacin is likely to be the recommended therapy particularly in areas with multi-resistant strains. In general, no antibiotic should be given prophylactically to protect against enteric fever or gastroenteritis
Food poisoning and gastroenteritis	Consult microbiologist or infectious diseases specialist. Antimicrobials are seldom indicated. Erythromycin (oral) may be of use in *Campylobacter* infection
Gall bladder and biliary infections	Piperacillin/tazobactam **or** Cefotaxime **plus** amoxycillin **or** Ciprofloxacin **plus** amoxycillin
Intra-abdominal sepsis (peritonitis, abscess)	Gentamicin **plus** benzylpenicillin **plus** metronidazole **or** Ciprofloxacin **plus** amoxycillin **plus** metronidazole

Infections in gynaecology and obstetrics

Abscess, Bartholins/labial	Surgery Co-amoxiclav *or for gonorrhoea and chlamydia* Ceftriaxone **plus either** doxycycline or azithromycin **or** Ciprofloxacin **plus either** doxycycline or azithromycin
Bacterial vaginosis	Metronidazole
Mastitis	Flucloxacillin
Pelvic inflammatory disease	Azithromycin or doxycycline **plus** metronidazole **plus** ciprofloxacin or ceftriaxone
Puerperal and post abortal sepsis	Gentamicin **plus** benzylpenicillin **plus** metronidazole **or** Piperacillin/tazobactam **plus** gentamicin or meropenem **plus** azithromycin *for chlamydia infections*
Trichomoniasis	Metronidazole

Sexually transmitted diseases

Chancroid	Ceftriaxone **or** Ciprofloxacin
Chlamydial infections (cervicitis, vaginal discharge, pelvic inflammatory disease, lymphogranuloma venereum)	Doxycycline **or** Azithromycin

Cont'd.

Uncomplicated gonorrhoea	Ciprofloxacin **or** Amoxycillin **plus** probenicid **or** Co-amoxiclav **plus** probenicid **or** Ceftriaxone
Complicated gonorrhoea	Benzylpenicillin **or** Ceftriaxone or cefotaxime **or** Ciprofloxacin *Note* Physicians must be aware of local sensitivity patterns. Quinolones must not be prescribed in children or growing adolescents
Granuloma inguinale	Doxycycline **or** Ciprofloxacin **or** Azithromycin
Syphilis	Procaine penicillin

Acute bone and joint infections

Take blood cultures and synovial fluid as appropriate before starting empirical antibiotic treatment	*Children under 6 weeks* Cefotaxime **or** Cefuroxime *Other patients* Ceftriaxone **or** Cefotaxime *Note* 1. Seek microbiological/orthopaedic advice, especially in chronic infections or where a prosthesis is in place. Flucloxacillin **plus** ciprofloxacin (not in children) **or** Piperacillin/tazobactam may be appropriate 2. In known *Staphylococcus aureus* infection prescribe flucloxacillin **plus either** gentamicin or fusidic acid 3. When bacteriological results become available antibiotic treatment may need to be reviewed

Central nervous system

***Haemophilus influenzae* meningitis**	Ceftriaxone **or** Cefotaxime **or** Chloramphenicol
Listeria meningitis	Amoxycillin **plus** gentamicin
Meningococcal and pneumococcal meningitis	Benzylpenicillin **or** Ceftriaxone **or** Cefotaxime
Pyogenic meningitis (unknown cause)	Ceftriaxone **plus** amoxycillin *or in neonates* Cefotaxime **plus** amoxycillin
Post-surgical meningitis	Seek specialist advice
Subdural empyema	Seek specialist advice
Suppurative intracranial phlebitis	Seek specialist advice
Brain abscess	Seek specialist advice
Epidural abscess	Seek specialist advice

Septicaemia/sepsis syndrome

Community-acquired infection in non-neutropenic patients (neutrophil count > 1 x 10⁹/l)

(a) *Suspected urinary tract source*
Ceftriaxone or cefotaxime **plus** gentamicin **plus** amoxycillin
or Ciprofloxacin **plus** gentamicin
(b) *Source other than urinary tract*
Gentamicin **plus** amoxycillin **plus** metronidazole
or Ceftriaxone or cefotaxime **plus** amoxycillin **plus** metronidazole

Infection in a neutropenic patient

Ceftazidime **plus** gentamicin **plus** metronidazole
or Ciprofloxacin **plus** gentamicin **plus** metronidazole
or Piperacillin/tazobactam **plus** gentamicin

Hospital-acquired infection in a non-neutropenic patient – recommendation as in (b) above

Notes
1. If infection is thought to be associated with an intravascular device or foreign implant add Vancomycin **or** Teicoplanin
2. If *Staphylococcus aureus* infection is likely add flucloxacillin
3. If pseudomonal infection is likely choose a regime recommended for neutropenic patients
4. Antifungal agents may be required. Seek specialist advice

Cardiovascular system

Endocarditis due to penicillin-sensitive streptococci	Benzylpenicillin **or** Benzylpenicillin **plus** gentamicin
Endocarditis due to penicillin-resistant streptococci	Benzylpenicillin **plus** gentamicin
Endocarditis due to *Staphylococcus aureus*	Flucloxacillin **plus** gentamicin **or** Flucloxacillin **plus** fusidic acid by mouth
Endocarditis due to coagulase-negative staphylococci	Vancomycin **plus** another antibiotic recommended by a microbiologist **or** Flucloxacillin **plus** gentamicin *Note* For patients hypersensitive to β-lactams use vancomycin or teicoplanin. The bacteriology laboratory will suggest a second antimicrobial

Superficial fungal infections

Cutaneous candidosis	Topical clotrimazole **or** Miconazole with hydrocortisone
Oral candidosis	Nystatin suspension or pastilles **or** Amphotericin oral suspension or lozenges **or** Miconazole oral gel **or** *in HIV patients* Fluconazole by mouth
Vaginal candidosis	Topical clotrimazole **or** miconazole **plus** *in recurrent infections* intermittent fluconazole by mouth

Cont'd.

Otomycosis	Topical nystatin suspension or ointment or gel **or** Econazole nitrate cream
Tinea capitis	Terbinafine Topical clotrimazole **or** miconazole
Tinea corporis/cruris	Itraconazole **plus** topical clotrimazole or miconazole
Tinea pedis/manuum	Topical clotrimazole or miconazole **or** *if severe* Itraconazole by mouth
Tinea unguium	Terbinafine **plus** topical amorolfine or tioconazole
Nail infections (moulds)	Nail removal is often necessary Topical imadazole cream Itraconazole by mouth

Index

Page numbers in *italic* refer to the illustrations